The Talk About "From Tragedy to Triumph"

After reading *From Tragedy to Triumph*, my eyes were opened and my heart was flooded with gratitude to God for being so loving and merciful to me. As I journeyed through the book and relived many of the moments, I realized that I had been walking in my own strength instead of asking God to carry me in His everlasting arms. With tears streaming down my face, God brought a final release and acceptance of the love that Pamela and Kirk have shown to me every day since the tragedy. God is ever merciful and loving and does indeed heal the broken-hearted.

This book will demonstrate to you the power of God to carry you through the most devastating circumstances. Pamela's testimony reveals that God does indeed show Himself to be faithful and strong to His children. She encourages you to seek God in prayer every step of the way and He will make you stand and above all else — stand.

~ **Deborah Powell,** Author's Mother, New Hope Church, Pearland, TX

There is more to this book than what the title reveals. The transparency in *From Tragedy to Triumph* will bring deliverance and healing to all who read it. As you journey with Pamela, she takes you through the Scriptures and demonstrates how to apply the Word to your life and see manifestations of His glory. She shows you how to submit, yield, surrender and humble yourself under the mighty hand of God and how to employ your Helper, Comforter, Leader, and Guide — the Holy Spirit. You will see how God brought growth through this tragedy and will be encouraged that He can do the same for you through anything that comes your way.

This book is easy to read, understand, and apply the principles to any situation you are facing. Get ready for your expectations to be exceeded. You will experience God in such a profound way as Pam illustrates how to cultivate a relationship with Him through spending time in the Word, prayer, and quiet time before Him. You will gain wisdom, insight, clarity, understanding, and strength to keep walking even through losing a child and to trust God through the process so you can come out of the fire without being burned or carry the stench of smoke.

Victory is inevitable! So, grab your Kleenex, notepad, and pen and get ready for a journey that will leave you encouraged, inspired, and ready to cultivate a relationship with God that will leave you empowered, satisfied, fulfilled, and wanting more of Him. This book points you to The Trinity (Father God, Jesus, and Holy Spirit) and lets you know you need them every day. Well done, Pam! God is surely pleased and gets all the glory.

~Minister Tamela Wynn,
The Potter's House North, Dallas, TX

The book, *From Tragedy to Triumph*, by Pamela Thompson is truly profound and needed in this season of my life. I recently lost my 20-year-old daughter in a head-on collision. Oftentimes we hear, "I know how you feel," and most of the time it's from people who have never lost a child. This book speaks to me because Pamela can relate to what I am going through. Secondly, she is so transparent which I love because in a person's openness, one can walk away with the thought of, "Wow, I am not alone." Thirdly, *From Tragedy to Triumph* is filled with the Word of God that comforts me in my current situation and grieving process. Lastly, this book moves one into the author's testimony which is her triumph. This gave me hope because God is not a respecter of persons — if He pulled her out of her tragedy and brought her into triumph — He is well able to do the same for me.

~Dr. Verrick Norwood, *Pastor,*
Holy Temple Christian Center, Victorville, CA

From Tragedy to Triumph has blessed me in so many ways. Having just recently lost my 20-year-old daughter in a car accident myself, this book hit me right in my heart, spirit, and soul. Reading that someone else has gone through a similar situation as myself is one thing but to read the book and say, "Wow, that's just how I feel," or "Wow, that's what I said," or "Wow, I was wondering if God would do that for me" is another thing. This book brings healing and encouragement that there is hope in God to get through this unbelievably difficult time.

Every Scripture spoke volumes to me, especially Proverbs 3:5-6 because, during a time like this, it is sometimes difficult to trust God when your heart is broken into a million pieces and you are trying to make sense of what just happened. Psalm 46 and Psalm 34 speak of the Lord being a present help in time of need and being near to the brokenhearted. At times, it was hard for me to grasp because my mind was thinking, "How is it that my daughter is gone?" This book gave me a better perspective to know that God is right there with me comforting me and that I just have to let go and receive His comfort.

What I have taken away from this anointed book is that it does not matter what situation we face in life — be it the devastating loss of a child, the ending of a marriage, the loss of worldly possessions, illness, etc. — one thing is certain and that is that God does not change. Neither does His unconditional and unfailing love for us, nor His ever-presence in our lives, along with His unrelenting desire to help us through every difficult situation and circumstance of life that we try to get through on our own but can't.

I have learned that God is not an option but a necessity if I am going to get through losing my child.

Without Him, it will never happen. Thank you for sharing your story and giving me the hope that the Lord will answer the questions that I have instead of leaving me in the dark, confused and weary. Thank you for showing me that the enemy meant for this tragedy to break me, but God is going to turn it around and make me into the woman He ordained me to be. Thank you for giving me something to look forward to.

~**Mecheco Norwood,** Co-Pastor,
Holy Temple Christian Center, Victorville, CA

From Tragedy to Triumph succeeded at two things. First, as the book started out, all parents have thoughts about the extreme difficulty in losing a child. In the book, Pam has blessed us with a window into her soul as she learned how to walk through such a tragedy.

Secondly, this book successfully points to the ultimate source of hope and peace — God. With this, my heart is left with a renewed confidence in the power of God, especially for those who suffer.

As Pam stated, "When someone shows you who they really are, believe them." Although this was referring to the reality of her husband and his challenges with being the spiritual leader of their home, I also think this is ultimately what this book is saying about God. When God shows you who He is, believe Him! I'm amazed at the numerous specific ways the Lord encouraged Pam, from the video from the night of prayer to the dream He gave her of Kiara pulling up in a limousine. I'm left in awe of the faithfulness of God.

I believe this book has the unique ability to truly help people experience triumph after any tragedy, whether it's the loss of a child or not. Pam masterfully gives us all that we need from Scriptures to prayers to fully rest in God's unchanging hand. Because of this book, I'm experiencing deeper healing after having walked through my own tragedies. For that, I am deeply grateful to Pam for writing it and recommend anyone and everyone to slowly read it and let God amaze you!

*~ **Pastor Curtis Gilbert**, Lead Pastor, The Journey Metro East, journey.org/me, Belleville, IL*

This book is an absolute must-read for anyone who has tragically lost a child or loved one. How does someone survive the death of a child? Pam reveals how as she completely opens and shares her heart and life. She shines the light of truth on her past, her family, and her pain. Her transparency is extraordinary! There are moments in this book when you will cry. There are other times when you will smile and laugh. There are times when... you will gasp!

You are guaranteed to walk away knowing that you can survive and thrive after such a devastating loss. Let Pam be the beam of light that guides you through the devastation and darkness. In this book, she is a projection of light energy radiating from the

Light source of God. She shines the light on God's grace, mercy, and loving-kindness. She illuminates His infinite reservoir of peace and comfort. Your soul will be uplifted. Your faith will be encouraged and your life will be forever changed.

*~ **Francesca Crain (Ms. Shonnie)**,*
Nursery Family, Beaumont, TX

The devastating loss of a child is unimaginable. It is our job as parents to properly steward over our children, understanding the precious gifts from God that they are, so to have one transition from this life into eternity prior to us, can be a lot to bear.

As a pastor, mother of five, and what I believe to be a woman of faith, I still have challenges with warding off the anxiety, fear, and concern that often accompanies parenting. Sometimes, it is a constant battle to maintain the peace of mind that only God can give while trusting in His sovereignty, goodness, and unconditional love to watch over them. When the battle in my mind is fierce, it has been this trust in Him that has been my chief sense of solace, help, and encouragement.

Throughout the pages of her compelling story, Author Pamela Thompson not only displays her unwavering trust in God but reveals to readers that they too can find hope even during the most difficult of times. Jesus told us that we would have tribulation in life. Tragedy is not a matter of "if" but "when" and our ability to triumph despite it is found through the lessons learned and the courage exemplified in this book.

*~ **Dr. Kisia L. Coleman**,*
M.O.D.E.L. (Mentoring Our Daughters, Equipping Ladies) Ministries, Founder, Kingdom Church Int'l., Co-Founder, KishKnows, Inc., Book Publishing Coach & Self-Publishing Servicer, Chicago, IL

FROM TRAGEDY TO TRIUMPH

FINDING HOPE, HEALING, & FREEDOM AFTER LOSING A CHILD

PAMELA THOMPSON

From Tragedy to Triumph – Finding Hope, Healing, & Freedom After Losing a Child
by Pamela Thompson

Cover design, editing, book layout and publishing services by KishKnows, Inc., Richton Park, Illinois, 708-252-DOIT
admin@kishknows.com, www.kishknows.com

ISBN 978-0-9998612-0-2
LCCN 2018901907

All rights reserved. No part of this book may be reproduced, distributed, or transmitted in any form or by any means, including photocopying, recording, digital scanning, or other electronic or mechanical methods, without the prior written permission of the publisher, except in the case of brief quotations embodied in critical reviews and certain other noncommercial uses permitted by copyright law. For permission requests, please contact Pamela Thompson.

Some Scripture references may be paraphrased versions or illustrative references of the author. Unless otherwise specified, all other references are from the Hebrew-Greek Key Word Study Bible, New King James Version® (NKJV). Copyright © 1982 by Thomas Nelson. Used by permission. All rights reserved.

Scripture quotations marked (TLB) are taken from The Living Bible, Copyright © 1971. Used by permission of Tyndale House Publishers, Inc., Carol Stream, Illinois 60188. All rights reserved.

Copyright © 2018 by Pamela Thompson

Printed in the United States of America

Dedication

I dedicate this book to all those who have lost a child in any circumstance and have dealt with the trials and tribulations of life. To those that do not know God or do know Him but didn't allow Him to carry them through the storms that came along with the loss, I hope you are encouraged to allow God to carry all your cares and deliver you from the grief and sorrow that accompanies the loss of a precious child.

We may not share the same circumstance as to how our child may have left this earth, but we share the fact that they are no longer with us and I want you to know that the only way to deal with it and continue to live life is to allow God to be your everything in this time. He can be your shoulder to cry on, your answer to the questions you have, your comforter, your teacher, and your guide through all the emotions that you will feel. He will be the lifter of your head when you can't physically lift it yourself, the reason you wake up every day after the loss and choose to live, and the only person that can mend your broken heart when you don't know what to do, think, or how to feel. He can fill the empty space in your heart with His unmatched love.

To the supporting cast of family members and friends that help us get through the tough times — just be there as a listening ear or a warm heart that we can lean on when we don't know what else to do.

I dedicate all the love that God has planted inside me for everyone that knows what this loss feels like. I hope that you can feel His love as you read this obedience book that He has placed on me to write, to deliver you all from the pain of grief and sorrow. Don't let it overtake you but trust God to heal you and deliver you out of the darkness of grief, and into His marvelous light of freedom and liberty to live on.

"And God will wipe away every tear
from their eyes,
there shall be no more death,
nor sorrow, nor crying.
There shall be no more pain,
for the former things have passed away."
(Revelation 21:4)

In Loving Memory

In remembrance of my amazing daughter, Kiara, who taught me how to Trust God for everything and the beauty of His unwavering and matchless LOVE for His children.

Table of Contents

Dedication xvii
In Loving Memory xxi
Introduction 1
Chapter One: Shaky Foundations 7
Chapter Two: The Father to the Fatherless 25
Chapter Three: The Hand of God 37
Chapter Four: The Tragedy 45
Chapter Five: Letting Go & Letting God Be God 67
Chapter Six: Hope Revealed 81
Chapter 7: The Triumph 97
Conclusion 111
Steps to Turn Tragedy into Triumph 119
Acknowledgements 121
About the Author 129
Contact the Author 131

Introduction

"The Spirit of the Lord God *is* upon Me,
Because the Lord has anointed Me
To preach good tidings to the poor;
He has sent Me to heal the brokenhearted,
To proclaim liberty to the captives,
And the opening of the prison
to *those who are* bound;
To proclaim the acceptable year of the Lord,
And the day of vengeance of our God;
To comfort all who mourn,
To console those who mourn in Zion,
To give them beauty for ashes,
The oil of joy for mourning,
The garment of praise for the spirit of heaviness;
That they may be called trees of righteousness,
The planting of the Lord, that
He may be glorified."
(Isaiah 61: 1 – 3)

Have you ever thought, "Wow, I wonder how people make it through losing a child?" And you ask God, "How do they do it?" He then tells you that without Him, they don't; and you wonder why you are even thinking like this or about this. The next thing you know, you are faced with this reality and walk out this process of losing your own precious child. Be careful what you ask God because the devil also hears you and comes to kill, steal, and destroy the plans you have and alter them completely when allowed to. Unexpectedly, you might just find yourself getting the answer to your question by living example — as I did.

I don't think I was quite prepared for what I was about to go through, but God knew that I would trust Him and allow Him to carry me all the way through that storm in my life. I was going on in life, seeking God for answers to my purpose and His plan for my life when He told me He was preparing me for something big. I was involved in the children's ministry, the nursery department at our church, and I had just begun to teach the class for three to five-year-olds. I was so nervous because I had never been the lead teacher before, only the teacher-helper, and the best snack preparer ever, in my opinion. God had called me to come from the back and teach the children the Word of God when I didn't have any training to teach at all. I had embraced that role as lead teacher so, thinking back, when I asked God about my purpose and He said He was preparing me for something big, I thought that was it.

I really began to get into it and started studying the lessons and creating puppet shows to go along with the lessons with my teacher-helper who became a close friend. Little did I know that God had other plans. The nursery department in my church was more like a close-knit family and we all got along so well. We didn't take it lightly that we were all called to minister to the precious children in such a way that they knew God on an intimate level even at their tender ages. In the process of me studying these lessons to minister to the children, I learned about important characters in the Bible and saw how God moved in the lives of the believers and nonbelievers in such a profound way.

In the meantime, my own daughter, Kiara, was part of the children's ministry and just as I was being transformed by the washing of the Word over me, she was getting the same washing. I began to notice her reading her children's Bible and quoting Scripture. She began to tell all her little friends about this Jesus that she was coming to know and love, with such sweetness and innocence that it was very moving to see. She would invite her cousins and friends to church with her because she wanted them to know this Jesus that was transforming her life in such a great way. My little angel started to pay attention to her words and how she was behaving. She also began to really pay attention to the behavior of others and especially to her father's behavior that she had always known was not right, but she didn't know how to help him until she met Jesus when she accepted Him as her personal Lord and Savior at the tender age of six.

This is where my story begins, so come along on this journey of how Jesus took me from tragedy to triumph — His way.

Chapter 1

Shaky Foundations

"Where can I go from Your Spirit?
Or where can I flee from Your presence?
If I ascend into heaven, You are there;
If I make my bed in hell, behold, You are there.
If I take the wings of the morning,
And dwell in the uttermost parts of the sea,
Even there Your hand shall lead me,
And Your right hand shall hold me."
(Psalm 139: 7 - 10)

You know, I never thought that I would bury my child. I always thought that my children would bury me. This little sweet angel of mine came to me at the tender age of twenty. I was so not ready to be a mom but my actions did not show that to be the case because I was doing what it took to become pregnant. I have no one to blame for this happening to me but myself because I knew better; but my flesh got the best of me when I met this young man that caused me to feel a certain kind of way. I met him at a time when I was vulnerable to the fact that there were some things in my life that I let happen, that I couldn't believe I had let happen because I was smarter than that but such is life. I had to rethink some choices and come up with a plan to do something with myself after graduating high school and returning back home after my freshman year of college.

You see, I went off to college — all fresh-faced and ready to conquer the world — but never bargained on college being so difficult for me. I was extremely, shockingly homesick because I was a momma's girl and I would cry every time she left after a visit to my college campus.

In college, your instructors don't care what you have going on in your life. They don't care if you show up or not because in a class with three hundred students, there is no roll call. All they consider is work turned in and tests that are taken. I was not focused on my classes at all because I missed my mom a lot and was trying to maintain my grades despite being so homesick. That did not fare so well because after the first semester, I had a D in history and another class because I didn't enjoy them and they were heavy reading courses, and I just didn't apply myself. I did okay in all my other classes but, after my first year, I needed to return home to regroup and figure things out. I decided to stay home and attend cosmetology school since I had been doing hair since I was eight or nine years old. I was braiding and combing my little cousins' hair for their moms and I really enjoyed it.

While I was attending cosmetology school, I became really good friends with one of the students and she introduced me to her boyfriend's best friend. This was when things became all too real with feelings and emotions that I had, that I did not put into proper perspective. So, I let my flesh rule and reign in my life.

This young man made me laugh and we had a good time together. We became a couple really quickly. We were having a good time with each other and he wanted things to get "hot and heavy." At first, I wasn't ready for all of that but as he persisted, I eventually succumbed to the pressure.

One day, I discovered that I was pregnant. I was devastated even though I knew that I was participating in an activity that could cause me to end up that way. I told him the news and he said, "Well, do you want to keep it?" Without even thinking, I replied, "Of course!" In my household, we didn't believe in abortion. I had made my bed and I knew I had to lie in it. I tried to figure out how I was going to tell my mom. She had warned me not to fall into the same trap that she did, and she knew that she didn't want that for her girls. I talked to my twin sister and asked her to speak to mom, but she said, "No way. You have to tell her yourself." I mustered up the courage and told my mom. She was disappointed but understanding at the same time.

I began to face the reality that becoming a mom was happening and I had to prepare my mind and my life. I graduated from cosmetology school before falling pregnant and I had enrolled in community college. I attended up until it was time to deliver my baby girl. By the way, I had to inform my instructor that I had missed my final exam because I was delivering my daughter! He said, "What?! You were pregnant?" I brought her to college to show him that I had indeed had a baby. He let me take the exam over the summer to complete the course.

The princess arrived and life was a whole lot different. It was a new experience being a mom versus being a young adult and only having to care for myself. I had this little person that needed me to do everything for her, and I was overwhelmed but in a good way. She gave me a reason and a cause to be and do better for myself and to provide for her. I was still with my daughter's father and things were financially difficult for us both. I remember one time when I told him that she needed diapers and he said that he didn't have any money. I said to him, "Oh, no... you got the wrong one buddy because this was a joint effort and if you don't take care of her, you won't see her!"

How many of you reading this know all too well that feeling of the father not showing up to take care of his responsibility? You see, this was what my mother was trying to protect me from because my dad was not in my life; he chose to live as if I didn't exist. Thankfully, this was the only occurrence of this happening with my daughter's father. He didn't want his daughter to grow up without him because, just like me, he didn't have his dad in his life either. This little girl caused her dad to grow up and do better for himself and for her. He didn't want her to have the life he or I had where we did not have a mom and a dad in our lives together, so we tried our best to make the relationship work. It was not an easy thing because we were raised differently. I had morals and values and I was raised in the church all my life; whereas he went to church but he didn't pay attention to what was being said from the pulpits. His mom allowed him to do whatever he wanted because she was working and he had to make sure his little brothers were taken care of when he should have been able to be a kid. We both stepped into some adult things before we were equipped or ready to do so — we were only in our early twenties. I had no real example of how to make a relationship work and neither did he, so we made a lot of mistakes.

I guess we thought that our baby girl could make everything work but in reality, it just complicated things. I was ready to settle down and become a family; however, he wanted to be young, wild and free yet still hold us on the side. It caused many conflicts between us. Yet, I was the glue that was holding everything together when it should have been a joint effort. Despite the conflict, the one thing we knew was when we saw this little baby's face, the world just seemed brighter and she caused us to overlook some things to give her the life we never had. The funny thing was, how do you give someone something that you didn't have or have ever seen modeled in front of you? It was the one thing we didn't think about.

As she was growing and getting bigger, so did our disagreements and arguments. At one stage, I decided that I wanted to call it quits and so did he, but that didn't last long because we knew we loved each other and we wanted to try to make things work.

However, we both wanted things to go *our* way and we all know how that story ends — more conflict.

We became engaged and I ended up compromising on what I knew to be right, and we moved in together before we were married. We were engaged without knowing what it took to have a successful relationship, so how in the world could we manage a successful marriage?

In the process of planning our wedding, I woke up one day and told him I could no longer live with him without being married. I felt that the Lord was telling me that I knew better and that I should wait until after the wedding to move in with him. But when I told him, he said, "Then, let's just go to the courthouse because I got this apartment for you and her to be with me and not me by myself." So, we went to the courthouse and got married. That was not what we needed to do because we had no clue on how to be married. Right before we got married, we joined this church together and started attending. When we told the pastor we wanted to get married, we thought they would have us go through some counseling but he just said, "Tell me where to be and what time to be there." We were both amazed but the wedding didn't happen anyway because, like I said, we went to the Justice of the Peace and got it done in minutes. It just so happened we were married around the time when Princess Diana had died and when I was watching all the stories about her life and her marriage to Prince Charles, that I found myself wondering, "What have I done? If the prince and princess couldn't stay married, what was I in for?"

We started off having difficulties because he wanted things his way and I wanted to do things my way. However, despite the difficulties, we always looked at Kiara and said we wanted it to be better and different for her. Our parents couldn't do it for us, so we had to make it work; we had to try and make it for her.

We all know that a child cannot hold a marriage together; only two people who are willing to put the other person first and choose to make it work. I felt like I was the one making all the sacrifices for this marriage because, at that time, my husband was immature and wanted to live as if he were single. I attended marriage classes alone and church alone for that matter. He attended church with my daughter and me when we were dating, but then once we were married, he started going less and less until he stopped going altogether. This put a real strain on our relationship because he was living in the world and doing things that were not right, and I started to withdraw myself from him and the marriage. I felt as if it was just me and my daughter.

She was getting even older and we were growing further apart as a couple. All I wanted was to have a happy marriage and family and he just wanted to live the life he felt he lost due to getting married so young. He would always say that he felt that he missed out on the single life and wondered what it would have been like to live on his own without the family package. I finally got to the point where I said, "If you want to find out, then let's get divorced and you go out there and see what that life is all about." He felt that he could find that out but still be married so we didn't get a divorce and then infidelity crept in. I couldn't believe that he would betray our covenant we made to God and each other. He felt justified because I was not affectionate towards him at all because, you see, he had betrayed my trust before we were married and I forgave him and married him anyway. When someone shows you who they really are, believe them. See, God told me not to get married when I did but I got married anyway. At that season in our relationship, I was seeing the results of my disobedience in the worst way — we were living in the same house but were very much separate.

I never thought that I would be married like that but it was not surprising because that's the type of household I grew up in. I never saw my parents show affection towards each other or have normal, meaningful conversations. I couldn't model a behavior that I was not familiar with, even though I tried. I always saw myself having the "Leave it to Beaver" type of household where the wife stayed home and took care of the house and family, and the father worked to support the family. I had that to some extent because my husband did take care of the financial aspects of our life. I just didn't have the right communication with my husband; I just shut down because I was tired of saying the same thing over and over. I kept telling him that we needed to go to counseling together because things were getting so out of hand, but he would ignore me or would say, "Black people don't do counseling, that's what White people do!" I tried going to counseling by myself but it only made me angrier because I felt as if I was trying and he wasn't. I didn't know how to love someone that betrayed me the way he did. Lord knows I tried; but when trust is broken, it's not an easy fix.

Just as I was getting over the broken trust of the past, I had found some emails that ended up coming to my mailbox instead of his; and he couldn't deny it. I was devastated and couldn't even look at him. But then God began to show me how *I* had allowed this to happen because I wasn't doing what I was supposed to. There were so many times that He told me to love my husband through his hurts and pains, and I just did not do it for whatever reason I came up with as an excuse. I would refer back to my hurts and dismiss what God was telling me to do. I paid the ultimate price for this choice because my husband felt that he could do whatever he wanted and, for a while, he did. The sad part about it was that I had got to the point where I didn't care anymore.

Hope & Healing

To anyone who is going through this in your marriage, do not enter the covenant of marriage lightly because it is a big deal. If God is telling you to wait, do not rush into it because God intended it to be until "death do us part" not "until I feel like we cannot reconcile our differences" which is a big reason people cite for divorce. The covenant of marriage is important to God and you should enter in with the plan and the heart to make it work through all trials and obstacles.

Infidelity is a serious thing to deal with in marriage but with God, all things are possible. With prayer and the belief in God and His Word, He can turn any bad situation around and make all things work together for our good. God loves us and the covenant of marriage so much because He is a God of covenant and relationship. His intention for marriage was to show His love for us and show how He is love.

As Christians, we are created in the image and likeness of God and we are to look to Him and copy how He modeled commitment. Throughout the Bible, we see that God was committed to His bride, Israel. He loved her so much that even though she cheated on Him by having other gods before Him, disobeying His commands, and murmuring and complaining against Him, He forgave them time and time again and took them back.

I know it is hard when your spouse is unfaithful and fails you. When we realize that marriage is not just to fulfill our personal happiness but to glorify God because we are a reflection of Him, then we realize that the person we married may fail us because of that sin nature or lack of relationship with God. We can then think about the marriage vows of staying together through good or bad, in sickness or in health, for richer or poorer, and forsaking all others and realize that if we are a reflection of God then we *cannot* give up on our marriage. We can honor our commitment or covenant and fight for our marriages through God's strength and His Spirit as I did.

It was not easy but, after reading Ephesians 5:22-33, "Wives, submit to your own husbands, as to the Lord. For the husband is head of the wife, as also Christ is head of the church; and He is the Savior of the body," I realized that I was not doing all that these Scriptures commanded me to do, so I could not give up on something that I had not fully given my all to fulfill. I had to be a *doer* of the Word and honor the covenant of marriage.

God has brought restoration and healing to my marriage because the devil wanted Kiara's death to destroy it but it actually brought us closer together. We needed each other to get through this tough situation. We understood that for a lot of couples, the death of a child ended some marriages but we held on to God's unchanging hand and allowed Him to help us get through it.

We attended church as a family, prayed together, read the Bible together, and often communicated how we were feeling about the situation. Communication was the key and it was something that was lost but found during this time. What the devil meant for bad, God turned around for our good. Just know that I could not have forgiven my husband without God and His Word at work within me. Our marriage could not have survived this tragedy without Him drawing us to Him and binding us together.

"Though one may be overpowered by another,
two can withstand him.
And a threefold cord is not quickly broken."
(Ecclesiastes 4:12)

Chapter 2

The Father to the Fatherless

"O Lord, You have searched me and known *me*.
You know my sitting down and my rising up;
You understand my thought afar off.
You comprehend my path and my lying down,
And are acquainted with all my ways.
For *there is* not a word on my tongue,
But behold, O Lord, You know it altogether.
You have hedged me behind and before,
And laid Your hand upon me."
(Psalm 139: 1 – 5)

All through the seasons of my life, this one thing I know is that without the Lord on my side, I don't know where in the world I would be. Looking back,

I can see all the ways the Lord was there with me; protecting me from harm and from myself. I can see how He kept me when I didn't know what to do and how to get out of the ruts in life. God was there to pick me up when I didn't have a father figure to lean on or ask questions about situations and circumstances in life.

When I made the decision to have unprotected sex and became pregnant with my first child, I didn't blame God nor was that what He wanted for me. That was a decision that I had made but He helped me to forgive myself for that mistake, pick myself back up, and continue in school to graduate as a young mom. I decided to marry my daughter's father, now my husband, even though I felt that I wasn't ready and he wasn't ready either. God carried me through the rough times we had as a young couple with a child when in a sense, we were still children ourselves.

I had to allow God to be my Father because my biological dad was not in my life. That decision to give God that place in my life was the best decision I could have made because I just wasn't close to my stepdad. While growing up, I watched their relationship and the difficulties that they had, and I felt that the only One I could *really* trust was God. I had a hard time trusting men because I felt that most of the ones in my life had failed me tremendously. The trials and struggles that we went through in our early years of marriage broke me down the most. I shouldn't have allowed it; but I did.

Take a lesson from me: If the guy you are supposed to be exclusive with shows you that he is not faithful before you say "I do," don't move on with him unless you both get the counseling or help you need to figure out why it happened and the part *each* of you played in that occurring. Don't just brush it off and hope that it will get better without you *both* doing the work necessary. If either party shows signs of not wanting to work it out, please move on and don't put each other through the pain of only one person fighting for a relationship that will never work unless two agree that it is worth fighting for.

I know this because in the early years of our relationship, I lived through being the only one fighting for what my husband would constantly say he wanted, but his actions never lined up with his words. Let the actions of a person speak louder than their words because you teach people how to treat you. I taught him that the good Christian girl would forgive no matter what, yet I was bleeding on the inside from the stabs at my self-esteem, my trust that was broken, and the shattered belief that he would always protect my heart; that my husband would love me as Christ loved the Church and gave Himself for it, and that he would never intentionally do anything to hurt me.

I was wrong about believing that he would never hurt me because I now realize that people will hurt you and disappoint you. However, my beliefs about a believing husband's role were right. People are human and can and will make mistakes but as Christians, we are called to forgive. Although I wanted him to love me that way, I realized he did not know *how* to do that because he did not know what that really meant to love me like Christ loved the Church and gave Himself for it. How could he be and do something he did not understand?

The Lord has worked mighty things within our marriage and in both our hearts since then, but I can honestly say that during that season of our marriage, my husband showed me that he wasn't trustworthy. I was naïve and never had a man in my life to actually show me how to value my worth, so I just didn't make him respect me. That is another thing ladies; please demand respect from the beginning and when a man shows you who he is, believe him and walk away when you see the signs that he will not love, respect, and protect you.

I had many nights when I cried myself to sleep because I just couldn't believe that this was my life. I was a married woman but felt so alone. How does that happen? I can tell you, it happens when you have two people who have two different ways of thinking and they are both adamant that they have to have it *their* way and no other way. As the saying goes, "It takes two to tango" and I wasn't obeying what God had called me to do as a wife. He had called me to love my husband with His unconditional love through all his struggles. The Lord kept telling me that my obedience to Him was so worth the sacrifice of being the bigger person and laying aside the weight of always being the one to give in. I had to learn the hard way because I kept refusing to show love, especially when I felt it wasn't warranted because he was not right at all.

Do you know that in the end, God's way is always the best way? I am here to tell you that I caused myself so much heartache and pain because I wanted to do things *my* way. I would cast the care of my marriage on God and then if I felt that God was taking too long or I had come up with a better way, I would take it back from God and implement my idea of what my husband needed, to no avail. I cannot tell you how many wasted years I went through because I knew "better" than God, or so I thought. I was the "know-it-all" wife that did not know anything because I did not do what God had been instructing me to do for a man that He created, knew all about, and loved. I just kept justifying my disobedience as me wanting to have it *my* way, which I thought was the "right way" and "God, just punish my husband for not being right!"

> **"Has the Lord *as great* delight in**
> **burnt offerings and sacrifices,**
> **As in obeying the voice of the Lord?**
> **Behold, to obey is better than sacrifice,**
> ***And* to heed than the fat of rams."**
> **(1 Samuel 15:22)**

Let me just say, when you go to God about someone else, He gets you together instead! If I had only realized that God was on my side all along, I could have saved myself from a lot of things that I blamed on the devil but were actually my disobedience and my choices that got me the harvest of a bad marital relationship. I thought the "shutdown method" would work but, after so many years, why didn't the light bulb in my head go off? Actually, it did but I was just too blinded by my own self that I didn't see the illumination of it. I can honestly say, God had always given me a way of escape but I just didn't heed the warning signs because I wanted to be right in my own sight and not in God's sight. The Word says,

"There is a way *that seems* right to a man, but its end *is* the way of death."
(Proverbs 14:12)

God was showing me that if I didn't begin to follow His way instead of my own, it would lead to death.

Not a physical death but the death of my marriage. I had to be the one to do the heavy lifting in this relationship because I was the one really walking with the Lord at the time. My husband was confessing to being a Christian but his life didn't reflect that. God was so hard on me because He loves me — His beloved daughter. I was the one in the Word, praying and praising, seeking God and His Kingdom and laboring for my family. I would oftentimes get so angry that I was the spiritual head of my household when that was my husband's place. God had to often remind me that I knew what I was getting into when I married a man who didn't display the characteristics of a God-loving and God-fearing man from the beginning.

If a man or woman that you are considering to marry doesn't display the characteristics of a God-fearing and God-loving person and you are a Christian, then please don't be unequally yoked together with an unbeliever. It will cause you a lot of heartache and pain because what fellowship has righteousness with lawlessness? What communion has light with darkness? The Word is true when it says: "Do not be unequally yoked together with unbelievers. For what fellowship has righteousness with lawlessness? And what communion has light with darkness?" (2 Corinthians 6:14) Take it from me because I lived this way for a long time, it's so draining of all that you are in Christ.

Although my husband and I were saved together before we were married, I think he did it because it was what I wanted for us and he just went along with it. I will tell you that my God has been so patient with my stubborn self that He has changed, shaped, and molded me into a woman who now knows what it feels like to allow God to lead and direct my path in every area of my life. It didn't happen overnight but it could have happened sooner if I would have been obedient in the beginning. Thank you, Lord, for the grace and mercy You have shown me all of my life.

"Surely goodness and mercy shall follow me
All the days of my life;
And I will dwell
in the house of the Lord
Forever."
(Psalm 23:6)

Hope & Healing

Please be obedient to the Voice of God when He gives you instructions on how to make a relationship work for your good. Wait on the Lord when making a decision on who you should marry and do not rush the process. Isaiah 40:31 says:

"But those who wait on the Lord
shall renew their strength;
they shall mount up with wings like eagles,
they shall run and not be weary,
they shall walk and not faint."

When you wait on the Lord, you will dodge some unnecessary obstacles. He knows all and we do not. So, when He instructs you, it will cause no harm but only good when you follow His instructions. I realized, I was being disobedient because although I said I trusted God, I really did not or I would have followed His commands. Trust in the Lord because He loves you so much.

Chapter 3

The Hand of God

*"You have hedged me behind and before,
And laid Your hand upon me.
Such knowledge *is* too wonderful for me;
It is high, I cannot attain it."*
(Psalm 139:5-6)

As I journeyed with God, He started showing me how He had always been there for me through everything I experienced in my life. He went as far back as my childhood when I saw my parents argue and fight, and He protected us from being harmed. He showed me the many times that I had been around when there were people shooting and I didn't get hurt.

One particular time was when I was at a college party and a young teenager tried to get into the party, but the organization wouldn't allow him access. He left and came back with a gun. At more or less the same time that he returned, my friend had just asked me to go with her to the front of the venue, next to the door to join some other friends that were gathered there. However, my sister had come to visit me and happened to have forgotten her jacket inside and wanted me to go with her instead, so I went inside to the party room with my sister. We got her jacket; and as we were heading into the lobby to leave, we heard gunshots from outside. My sister and I turned to run back into the party room, but everyone was running out in a panic *towards* the gunshots, thinking that the shots were from inside the party room. We were trampled in the chaos. When all the madness died down, I found out that my friend — who had wanted me to go with her — was by the door when this guy came back. She ended up getting shot. She lost her eye in the process and God said to me, *"See, I protected you."*

I also remembered another time when my sisters and I were at a school dance and shots were fired. The security guard grabbed us and ducked into the bushes. We were protected again and God said, *"See, I protected you again."*

During the time leading up to the loss of my daughter, the Lord continued to show me how He had protected me. There were so many instances that He brought to mind that I became overwhelmed at the hand of God over my life. So, when the tragedy of my daughter came about, I couldn't do anything but allow Him to carry me.

"The eternal God *is your* refuge,
And underneath *are* the everlasting arms;"
(Deuteronomy 33:27)

In the beginning, I couldn't see the light at the end of the tunnel because He had me so covered that there were people who thought, "Surely her daughter didn't really die because she is behaving like nothing has happened." In reality, all I had done was cast my care on my God because He cared for me and He had shown me that I could trust Him with all my heart, lean not on my own understanding, and in all my ways acknowledge Him and He would direct my path. My God was showing me how He could take my sadness and sorrow and turn it into gladness right before my eyes. I was also trying to be strong for my husband because he was really having a hard time with the fact that our daughter was gone.

Meanwhile, I was praying to God that she would be raised from the dead and everyone would see that God was still in the miracle-working business. I had people who were standing with me in my belief that Kiara would get up and live. "My baby will live and not die, and declare the works of the Lord," was all I kept thinking in my head and heart. There was no way this was the end for my precious angel because she still had a lot of work to do — to bring souls into

God's Kingdom — because, at the time, she was in the middle of the Jesus Recruiter Program at church. She was on a roll asking her friends and family to come to church with her to hear about Jesus and how awesome He was. She was the top Jesus Recruiter at the time of her death and I was so proud of her. She had a boldness about herself when she talked about Jesus and how He wanted to make life better for everyone that accepted Him as their personal Lord and Savior.

I remember one particular time, our neighbor that she played with daily told her she had never heard a worship song. My daughter came running into the house, got her radio from her room and her favorite children's worship CD to play for her. That's the type of love she had for sharing the Lord with everyone. She could not understand how people wanted to live their life without Him. She really wanted to see her dad and her grandmother living their lives to the glory of God and she was on a mission to get them saved. She knew how amazing it was to be a child of God so she wanted any and everybody to be saved, especially those closest to her.

This shows you the heart of this little angel that God blessed our family with. At such a tender age, she knew that there was nothing like being in the family of God. I remember another incident where my husband's car was stolen while he was at a nightclub. When he came home and told her the next day, he couldn't believe her response. She said, "Dad, if you were at home with your family, you would still have your car," and she carried on eating her breakfast. That's how she was about the wrong choices he was making. The last thing she said to him before she left to go to the All Night Intercessory Prayer event with my mom was, "Dad, you know you shouldn't be drinking that beer. You should be going to church with Mom to pray." Little did we know that would be the last thing she said to him.

Hope & Healing

**"Casting all your care upon Him,
for he cares for you."
(1 Peter 5:7)**

God will always show up on your behalf when you give Him free reign to carry all of your cares. He wants to do this for everyone but you have to give Him permission to because He will not force Himself on anyone. Let Him show you that He will do what His Word says. Take the Scriptures and apply them to your life at all times and see how His hand moves over your life.

Kiara was speaking the truth to her dad when she told him that he should be going to church as well to pray with his family. Because that was the last thing she said to him, it had a big impact on him attending church after her death. If you are in a family and you are the head and you don't have a relationship with

God then now is the time to make that a priority in your life because you need Him to face all the trials and tribulations that life brings.

When you look back over your life, you can clearly see how God protects us even when we do not recognize it or acknowledge Him for doing so. Nothing in our lives happens by chance but because God loves the just and the unjust — He is in control of everything, even when we don't know Him.

Chapter 4

The Tragedy

> **"Yea, though I walk through
> the valley of the shadow of death,
> I will fear no evil;
> For You *are* with me;
> Your rod and Your staff,
> they comfort me."
> (Psalm 23:4)**

The night before Kiara went to be with the Lord, our church was holding the All Night Intercessory Prayer event that I mentioned earlier in this book. I want to tell you a bit about this amazing event that my daughter was so excited to be a part of so that you can understand the events leading up to her death... and the truths that were revealed after her death.

At the All Night Intercessory Prayer, there were several hundred people in attendance. There was a predetermined agenda and each ministry leader had a specific topic to pray about for several minutes in the main sanctuary. For example, they prayed for lost souls, salvation, being filled with the Holy Ghost, healing from sickness and disease, deliverance, the government officials, the President and his cabinet, schools, the homeless, teachers, businesses, and much more. This was arranged throughout the night, with breakfast provided in the morning.

The children's ministry was in the gym down the hall in the same building, and they had food and games for the children as well as a prayer agenda that was geared for children. For example, they would pray for those experiencing bullying or peer pressure or those children who were struggling with schoolwork.

When you walked into the gym, the first thing you saw was rows of chairs for the children to pray in and tables for eating. They had games set up behind the tables and chairs, but if you did not walk back there, you could not see the area from the doorway of the gym. You had to walk around the chairs and tables to see the games. They also had sleeping rooms set up in the classrooms down the hall from the gym.

Earlier that day, I was out shopping with my girls to buy them new clothes. Kiara and I were in the car singing our favorite worship songs. CeCe Winan's *Throne Room* had just come out and the song "Jesus, You are Beautiful" was our song. It came on and she would sing a verse and I would sing a verse. We also sang "From Mother to Daughter" from *Sacred Love Songs* by T.D. Jakes. I am so glad that God gave us that precious moment and time together because little did I know that would be the last time we would do that.

Kiara was so excited about going to the All Night Intercessory Prayer because I told her that she could spend the night there since my mom was volunteering to stay all night with the children's ministry team. They had to arrive early to set up so I got Kiara ready to leave early with my mom even though I tried to convince her to wait and ride with me and her baby sister; but all my efforts were to no avail. My mom was going to pick her up but asked if I could drop her off instead so she could get ready and take a little nap before they went, and so I did. Since I had made lasagna for my house, I packed some up for them to eat before they left for church and packed Kiara's sleeping bag and pillow and took her to my mom's house. While waiting for my mom to get ready, Kiara fell asleep and when she woke up, they went to the prayer event. Let me just tell you, my little girl prayed during the first fifteen minutes of every hour. My daughter prayed in the Spirit every time. Yes, you heard me right, my angel prayed in tongues.

The Tragedy

I was praying in the main sanctuary, holding my baby. During the breaks in prayer sessions, the leaders would tell the parents to check on their children. I went back during the breaks, three times in fact, but I didn't see her at all. I didn't know there was a games section and couldn't see anything from where I was standing. The people in the children's ministry were becoming frustrated with me asking them to figure out where my daughter was because I was so persistent. I didn't feel better about it until I saw my mom and she said that my daughter could be down the hall where the sleeping rooms were or also where they were praying because she got up to pray every time they called them to go and pray in the Spirit. I might have missed her in between the sessions.

When I looked back on the events of the night, I couldn't understand why I didn't see my daughter at all even though I went back there three times. God knows exactly why and didn't reveal it to me until after the accident.

I was engaged in the intercessory prayer and it was on fire. I could feel the presence of the Lord in the atmosphere. I was at a place in God that I will never forget because it was so peaceful all around me. I ended up leaving around one in the morning because my baby girl had finally fallen asleep. My baby hated driving and would cry the whole time because she could not see me. When she finally fell asleep, I decided to leave so that she wouldn't cry all the way home — it was a distance to drive. I had a difficult time driving home because I was so sleepy but I rolled the windows down and played worship music all the way home. My baby was fast asleep the whole way back. When I got home, I went straight to bed.

I was awakened by a call from the police at around 6am telling me that there had been an accident involving my daughter. I needed to go immediately to the hospital that was not too far from my house. I knew it was bad because my heart felt like it had dropped to my feet and I felt sick to my stomach. I looked up to Heaven and said, "Lord, help me with this because this is not good." I called my husband who had left for work not too long before and told him to come back home because there had been an accident involving Kiara. He arrived home so fast that I was still getting our baby girl ready.

On the way, we called my aunt who lived nearby to see if she could keep our baby girl but the hospital called on our way there and said, "Get here immediately!" So, we kept her with us and headed to the hospital. When we arrived, they told us that our daughter was not responding and said that we must talk to her and see if she responds to our voices — she didn't. I immediately felt my legs grow weak and I collapsed. The nurse caught me and my baby girl before we hit the floor. She said, "Be strong for your daughter." I had to call on the *one* name that I knew could carry me through the hurt and pain I was feeling — that name was Jesus. I said, "Lord, You will have to carry me through this because I can't even believe that what they are telling me is true. Lord, I am casting my care on You because You care for me and I do not know what to do except to pray that You heal her from the top of her head to the soles of her feet. You have the power to heal her and she will have nothing missing and nothing that's broken because one touch from You is all it takes to be made whole. Heal her right now, Lord, and show your miracle-working power to all these people in this hospital."

My husband was so frustrated with the hospital staff because they were not doing anything and he said, "Do something to help my daughter!" They began to put things in the IV and pump the breathing tube that was in her mouth, but nothing changed. I called one of the pastors from my church to come and pray and when he and his wife arrived, she said, "Anyone who does not believe in the miracle-working power of God raising someone from the dead must either leave the room or don't say anything at all!" She prayed and said, "Arise and walk, in the Name of Jesus!" My daughter just lay there so still as I held her hand and begged her to wake up and breathe. The man, who had arrived at the scene of the accident, said that he believed she took her last breath in his arms as he pulled her out of the car. All I kept hearing was, *"The breath of life is in this room."* I asked my husband, "Do you hear that?" and he said that he didn't hear anything. I just kept thinking that she would wake up and take a breath because I kept hearing it over and over.

We all finally left the hospital after they called a time of death and said there was nothing more they could do. They gave us the clothes she was wearing and asked us what mortuary we wanted to have her body released to. My husband took care of all of that because I just couldn't believe that she was gone.

When we finally arrived home, I went into my bedroom and prayed in the Spirit for what felt like an eternity. I had to call on the Name that I knew would get me through this tragic time in my life. I needed the Holy Spirit to comfort me, so I prayed in tongues until I felt the peace and comfort that only God could bring. I had a house full of people and they were knocking on my door but I desperately needed the Spirit of the Living God to build me up and equip me for what I was about to face. I prayed and cried, and cried and prayed, until finally, I felt the Lord say I was free to go and be with my family and friends. When I walked out of that room, they got a different me because I was full of the Holy Ghost and my Comforter had me in the palm of His hands the rest of that day and every day afterward.

When devastating events happen, as humans, we try to look for hope, bring words of comfort and try to understand why things happen. The day following her death, the church leaders told me that she woke up to pray every time they prayed. My stepdad said there was a glow around her as she slept at their house before she and my mom left to go to the All Night Intercessory Prayer and my mom even told me that the lasagna that I had made for them to eat before they went was the best one I had made for her. Initially, knowing these things brought little comfort — all I could think about at the time was the fact that I never saw her at church that night.

In the days following the accident, I had so many questions running through my mind but I just kept thanking God for my dead child being raised back to life like the children in the Bible that were raised back to life. I had such faith that God would do this for me because I was at the All Night Intercessory Prayer event the night before — giving Him praise and interceding for others as well as myself — so surely, the devil could not mess with me with all this oil and fire that was released through my prayers. How could this be that my child wasn't covered in prayer for this tragic incident to even occur? My mom was also at this prayer event praying. What went wrong that this was able to happen to her as well? She was only two blocks from her home when the accident occurred. Why would You, God, allow this to happen to two people who were praying in the Spirit all night long? I knew that the God I serve would not allow this to happen, but at the same time, nothing can happen if He does not allow it. "Why, my God, why did You allow this to happen to my innocent daughter?" This was the question that I couldn't get to leave my mind.

I couldn't even imagine what my husband was thinking because it was *my* mom who fell asleep at the wheel resulting in the accident. I even began to think that somehow, it was my fault because I didn't insist on Kiara leaving the prayer event with me because I didn't see her before I left the church. I had an uneasy feeling on the inside when I kept going back to the children's ministry to find her and did not see her.

Of course, the devil tried to play with my mind and make me think I had a part to play — but my God kept reassuring me that I had no hand in this tragic accident that had taken place. Of course, the devil was not going to give up that easy because he kept telling me I would lose my mind and, in my dreams, he showed me myself in a padded cell. My God is greater than the god of the world (Satan) because in that dream, the padded cell was bright white and God showed me that it was white because He was there in the midst of the room and wasn't going to allow the devil to have my mind. Every day I woke up and told that devil he could not have my mind because as long as I kept my mind stayed on the Lord, He would keep my mind in perfect peace. I'm so thankful that I knew the Word because it was what helped me stay in that Jesus-peace that surpassed all understanding.

> **You will keep *him* in perfect peace,**
> ***Whose* mind *is* stayed *on You*,**
> **Because he trusts in You.**
> **(Isaiah 26:3)**

I confessed God's Word often, every day because the devil comes to kill, steal, and destroy and he meant to do that to my mom, my husband, and myself. I would say, "Greater is He that is in me than he that is in the world" because Satan would tell me to curse God for doing this. I knew better because my God came so that I could have life and have it more abundantly and not kill me or my family. He is the God of family and He loves the family unit, that's why He created it. Satan wanted to get my focus off God so that he could pollute my mind into thinking I could not have a life without my daughter.

If the devil gets your mind, then he has *you*. The battlefield is the mind. The Word says, "Idle hands are the devil's workshop; idle lips are his mouthpiece" (Proverbs 16:27, TLB). Idle means to avoid work or to be lazy. It also means to have no purpose or to be pointless and the verb, the action word, means to spend time doing nothing. Idle hands and idle lips begin with an idle mind, a mind thinking about nothing and the devil wanted me idle. He wanted my mind to be numb but I kept my mind stayed on Jesus every step of the way. I woke up praying and went to bed praying because I knew that prayer changes things and I needed to stay in prayer for my entire family to get through this situation.

Despite praying continuously, I wanted to just stay in bed and hope I was dreaming and that I would wake up and my daughter would be in her room when I went into it but that wasn't the case. I had to come to the realization that my daughter was indeed gone from this life and her physical remains were at the funeral home, in a freezer. Yet, I continued to have faith that God would and could raise her from the dead.

My cousin and her husband who were pastoring their own church, came into town with the belief, like me, that my daughter would be raised from the dead. The three of us went to the funeral home to pray for my daughter to get up from her deathbed. I even have a brand-new outfit in a bag for Kiara to wear home.

The funeral home brought her body out for us to pray over her, and we did just that. As we are praying, the table upon which she was lying began to move and we got ready to see the manifestation of God raising her up. We continued to pray and the table carried on moving. It was so powerful, that one of the funeral home workers even began to pray with us. The owner of the funeral home came in and told her to come out of the room and said that she better not ever do that again. The worker was so upset that she yanked her arm from him before leaving the room.

We carried on praying and I remembered that on the way into the room to view my daughter, my cousin said, "The lady at the front desk is going to faint when she sees us come out of this room with your daughter alive and well again!" The table was still shaking and we thought that maybe we were leaning on it, causing it to move — we stepped away and the table carried on shaking! Then, all of a sudden, the table stopped shaking and we waited but nothing happened. So we left the funeral home feeling strange and disappointed because we knew what we believed God had told us all before we went to pray for her. I felt confused and questioned whether I had heard God say that the breath of life was in the hospital room and what it really meant. I took it to mean that she was going to be alive because the "breath of life" meant life to me. I ended up receiving the answer to this later on from the Lord, with a witness to confirm what happened.

The time came for me to face the facts that I really was planning the funeral of my beloved daughter. My husband and I, with some other family and friends, met with the funeral director to make arrangements and pick out a casket, which, by the way, I couldn't do. I let my husband go into the casket room and pick one and he made a lovely choice. I, on the other hand, was still believing that God would bring her back to life, so there was no need for me to pick a casket. While the meeting was going on, I was there in body but not really at all in spirit.

After meeting the funeral director, we met with the Bereavement Ministry at my church to get the program and the memorial service scheduled. I was in this meeting talking as if my daughter was not dead at all and the lady in charge of the ministry just acted as if I was not even there and proceeded to discuss all the details with my husband. Towards the end of the meeting, she told me to stop speaking as if my child was not dead because she was. I was stunned... and, at the time, I felt angry and hurt. Although I knew that Kiara was with the Lord, I still kept believing that she would come back and nothing else mattered to me. We loved her dearly and missed her so much. Looking back, I can see that during that time, we were still processing the shock and beginning to come to terms with the loss. I couldn't face the fact that Kiara was gone, and I had such faith that the Lord would bring her back.

After this incident, the head of bereavement then asked us to choose photographs for the obituary and bring them to her the next day. The meeting ended and we drove home in silence. I was trying to process the fact that my child was no longer with me.

My husband was so strong in planning all of this without me weighing in on any decisions at all. He went to the cemetery to choose a plot to bury her in and they told him that he needed six thousand dollars upfront because they did not do payment plans at this particular cemetery. He called my mom's insurance company because that's the car my daughter was in when the accident happened, but they told him that they have until she turned eighteen to pay out the claim. We were outdone because we did not have any life insurance for her life. We were so young at that time and didn't even think to buy life insurance for our child. Who thinks to buy life insurance for their kids? Since the accident, we have found out that many parents don't even think of making this provision of life insurance for themselves or their children. I encourage you, it *is* important because we don't know what the future may hold.

My husband discussed this problem with his mom and she suggested that he calls his car insurance company. Thankfully, they told him that they would pay for it and then claim it from my mom's insurance company. Our car insurance company even paid for the funeral costs! I thank God for this because He made a way out of no way.

> **"And my God shall supply all your need according to His riches in glory by Christ Jesus. Now to our God and Father *be* glory forever and ever. Amen."**
> **(Philippians 4:19-20)**

Hope & Healing

My hope was in the fact that I had to pray without ceasing in order to deal with this tragic loss. I prayed every morning when I woke up and every night before I went to bed and it helped me cope. I was given a book on grief and sorrow from my church and I read the Scriptures inside of it every day, and the Word was working as I worked the Word. I kept my mind stayed on Jesus and He kept me in perfect peace.

I had questions for God and I told Him exactly how I was feeling because the Word says you have not because you ask not (James 4:2). Do not allow anyone to tell you that you cannot ask God anything because you can. I asked because I wanted to know some things and, in His timing, He answered.

CHAPTER 5

Letting Go & Letting God be God

"But now, thus says the Lord,
who created you, O Jacob,
And He who formed you, O Israel:
"Fear not, for I have redeemed you;
I have called *you* by your name;
You *are* Mine.
When you pass through the waters,
I *will be* with you;
And through the rivers,
they shall not overflow you.
When you walk through the fire,
you shall not be burned,
Nor shall the flame scorch you."
(Isaiah 43:1-2)

The day before the funeral arrived, I woke up, prayed and quietened myself before the Lord so that I could start my day with Him once again carrying me. During the time before the funeral, I just spent time with family and kept my mind stayed on the Lord so that He could keep me in perfect peace because I needed that peace, which surpasses all understanding, to keep going. That morning, we were going to the wake, which was the viewing of my daughter before the funeral the next day.

As I was getting ready to leave for the wake, I looked up and said, "Here we go again, Lord. You got me, right?" He says, *"Of course. Because I never leave you, remember?"*

When I arrived, I felt so sad because I just did not want to believe that it was really happening. I went inside to see my daughter and my hairstylist had done an amazing job — she looked beautiful. There were so many people already there but they did not allow anyone in until my husband and I gave them our seal of approval, and we did so.

The people began streaming in for the viewing and there were many that I did not know, but I thought "Hallelujah, anyhow!" I was standing strong and greeting everyone that came by and they were constantly telling me that they could not believe how well I was holding up. I told them, "It's all God and none of me because I am crying on the inside."

After about an hour of greeting people, I needed to go to the bathroom. On my way back inside, a little girl that was in kindergarten and attended the same school as my daughter stopped me and told me that she wanted to tell me how Kiara always played with her at recess. She said that even when all the older kids would tease Kiara and say, "Why are you playing with the babies?" she would continue to play with her and taught her how to jump rope. This little girl's mother said that she forced her to bring her to the wake just so that she could tell me how nice Kiara was to her even when others did not want her to be. This was just a testament to the amazing person I knew my baby to be. The little girl also said she wanted to give me a hug because she knew I needed one after losing my child. I hugged her and thanked her and her mom for thinking of me and my family.

On the way back inside, I could hear whispers from people who didn't know me saying, "Why is she not crying?" and "Did she even love her daughter because she is acting like nothing has happened." I was crying loud on the inside, but my God was carrying me like He told me He would if I cast my cares on Him, which I did.

Despite feeling shocked at the lack of compassion from some of those people there, who didn't even know me, I had to carry on and comfort so many people who were devastated by this whole situation. It was a long night because I stayed for the entire two hours that they had her out for viewing. I was only able to do that because I was full of God and the Holy Spirit, and I allowed them full access to my soul, mind, body, and spirit. When it was finally over, I went home to relax; but when I got home, I was so drained that I went to bed.

I did not get much sleep because I was just so ready to see the miracle of her getting out of that casket and returning home with us. That night, I had a dream that she was brought to us in a limousine. She got out of the car and looked like an angel, all dressed in white. It was so vivid that I woke up, jumped out of my bed and looked out the window but I did not see the limousine so I went back to bed and fell asleep immediately.

> **"God *is* our refuge and strength,**
> **A very present help in trouble."**
> **(Psalm 46:1)**

The next morning, the funeral and burial were staring me in the face and I realized that it was going to be hard for me to say goodbye for now to my eight-year-old daughter, but easy if I continued to allow God to be my strength and my present help in my time of trouble as the Word of the Lord instructed me to let Him be in my life at that time. I woke up early and prayed in the Holy Ghost just to prepare myself for that miraculous day because I was still believing God for the miracle of Kiara being raised up from the dead at the memorial service. I got my baby and myself ready to attend the service. I could barely eat a bite of food because through this process, I couldn't swallow any food and it showed in the rapid weight-loss over that short period of time. I had to pin the pants of the outfit that I had purchased for them to stay up because they did not have belt loops.

As my husband and I prepared ourselves for this heartbreaking day, we prayed and people started to arrive at our home to attend the memorial service for our daughter. My heart was beating so fast the entire time. The pastor who was conducting the service arrived at our home to pray with our family before we went to the church. We greeted him and he prayed a powerful prayer, then we left for the church.

When we arrived at the church and saw my beloved daughter at the front of the church in her casket, I started shaking all over. As I walked down the center aisle with my twin sister right by my side, my mother called me over to her and so I went to her. She was in a wheelchair due to the injuries she sustained in the accident. My husband went to the other side of the church to sit down and she wanted to talk to him but I told her that it was not the time because he was also grieving, as we all were. She was grief-stricken and said, "Well, if he is not going to forgive me, okay." I told her that it was not like that. She just needed to give him time to process that tragic situation.

Before the service, one of my family members approached my daughter's casket and broke down to her knees. I went to console her and she got herself together as we prepared to start the service. Now, mind you, I gave the praise team free reign to choose the songs to sing at the service and they started with my daughter's favorite worship song from the children's ministry. My heart melted; they had thought of everything. I was the first one to my feet to sing along and praise my Lord singing "Every Move I Make" by *Shout Praises Kids* because my daughter played this song all the time. They played a few other selections and my mother-in-law read a poem she had written to Kiara. My husband also brought an awesome tribute to our little girl that I did not know he had prepared, and it was so touching. After his tribute, the message began. The pastor brought a word like no other to reach believers and nonbelievers alike, so much so that twenty-nine family members and friends received salvation at this service!

The service ended and we attended the repast, which is the gathering of family and friends to a meal after a funeral which my church provided. I heard it was delicious but I couldn't eat a thing, although I tried. I was there in body but my mind and my spirit were concentrated on the fact that I wanted my daughter to get up and walk out of that church with our family and show the miracle-working power of God but that did not happen.

We loaded up for the funeral procession to bury my angel and I was totally silent all the way to the cemetery. We arrived there and all I kept thinking was, "How am I going to walk away and leave my daughter behind?" I walked to the area where her casket was and I was shaking like a leaf. I looked up and I said to myself, "Lord, please help me. I need you right now." Next thing I knew, it was over and I was walking back to the car to head home without my child. I felt totally numb to everything but I had my family to entertain, so I pulled it together with

God's help and enjoyed the rest of the time with my family before they all headed back to their respective places out of town.

> **"The Lord is near to those**
> **who have a broken heart,**
> **And saves such as have a contrite spirit.**
> **Many are the afflictions of the righteous,**
> **But the Lord delivers him out of them all."**
> **(Psalm 34:18-19)**

Everyone went back home and my husband immediately returned back to work because it was what he needed to do to keep his mind off what we had just experienced. I was at home with my baby girl who was only eight months old at the time.

It was so amazing to see how smart she was because she went into her big sister's room and crawled around as if she was looking for her. As I watched her, I was amazed. She even lifted up the bed skirt on the bed and looked under the bed, and I started weeping because that baby knew that something was missing — it was her big sister.

You see, my daughter was so excited about being a big sister that she was like a second mother to her baby sister and loved her so much. She would wake in the night when her baby sister would cry because she hated to see her cry, and I would say, "Go back to bed because you have to get up for school in the morning." There were times I would need to get some things done around the house, so I would put the baby girl in her crib and sometimes she would cry and I would let her. But her big sister would be so mad at me! I would tell her, "She is okay to cry a little," but she wouldn't hear any of that. She was such an awesome big sister so, looking back, I can now see why my baby realized she was not there because she stayed in that baby's face all the time and would take her from anyone if she started to cry, even me and her dad.

When we left Kiara's room that day, I closed the door and did not open it until about a year later because it was hard for me to walk past it while open and not cry. I wanted Kiara to walk out as if nothing had ever happened. Every time I looked at that closed door, I would ask God to help me get past that emotional state of crying in grief and sorrow and move to joy and gladness before I open that door again.

As time moved on, we all continued to process the grief. My baby would go to the front door at the exact time Kiara would normally get home from school and I would look at the clock and think, "Wow, this is one smart baby." There would even be times where my baby girl would be staring up at the ceiling in the house and just laughing so hard, and my husband and I would say, "Her big sister is playing with her."

It took about a year before I could open that bedroom door again and I praised God like there was no tomorrow the day I finally opened it. It was not without tears, but they were happy ones instead of sorrowful ones this time. I had reached the point of healing where I had made up my mind that me seeing all the memories of her did not have to make me sorrowful anymore. I could rejoice in knowing she was with Jesus, in the best place to be and that was Heaven. I cleaned up the room and I felt her presence in there and I was finally able to make peace with her absence.

Hope & Healing

I would not have made it through without God being my strength and my refuge. For the weeks during and after this ordeal, I did not have an appetite. I literally had a hard time swallowing anything and I couldn't physically nourish myself. He carried me when my body was physically weak from lack of sustenance. He gave me strength when I had none. He was also my refuge — I could hide in Him when it all became too much.

Just me walking around was all glory to Him and He did it for me day after day until I was able to eat and drink and nourish myself. My God was, and is, awesome and I want the world to know it!

I allowed myself time to grieve even though I was told that it was not necessary to cry for her because she was with the Lord and she would not come back here for anything in the world. I did understand that there is nothing like the presence of the Lord but, at the time, when I was told that I shouldn't grieve because she was with Him, it didn't bring me comfort — I felt that it was insensitive and showed a lack of compassion for my pain and loss.

Prayer was the main ingredient for this process of letting go and letting God be God. I literally had to pray without ceasing. I did not want my own thoughts to get in the way of God taking full control of my thoughts, knowing that His thoughts are so much higher than mine. God allowed me to be in that place that would let Him prove Himself to be who He said He is in His Word and I was able to taste and see that the Lord is good.

Chapter 6

Hope Revealed

"But I do not want you to be ignorant, brethren, concerning those who have fallen asleep, lest you sorrow as others who have no hope. For if we believe that Jesus died and rose again, even so God will bring with Him those who sleep in Jesus."

(1 Thessalonians 4:13-14)

There were a few revelations that I got from God when all was said and done. The first revelation happened the day after the accident. One of the church youth leaders and his wife came to see us. He said that he wasn't planning to attend the All-Night Intercessory Prayer because he had some dental work done that day. However, he ended up going and filmed the whole night. They had brought the video to show me, not knowing that I couldn't find my daughter at the church the night before she died.

The first face you could see on it was Kiara playing Twister with some other children on the floor. She was smiling and laughing and having so much fun! Every time the camera filmed her, you could see her bright smile. My mom had told me that Kiara had a really good time and that even in the Bible quiz games, she kept on winning the prizes. When I watched that video, I could see for myself how happy she was that night and it brought me so much comfort. It also explained why I didn't see her when I went to look for her during the breaks. When I went to the children's ministry area, I had only looked at the chairs and tables set out for praying and eating. It didn't dawn on me to scan the activity area beyond the tables and chairs, so I didn't see her.

God is so good! He orchestrated it so that they brought that video over to show me just how much fun she was having before she left the Earth *and* He also answered my question as to why I didn't see her. The youth leader and his wife were so floored by God when I told them how much of a blessing the video was to me.

> "'Because he loves me,' says the Lord,
> 'I will rescue him;
> I will protect him,
> for he acknowledges my name.
> He will call on me, and I will answer him;
> I will be with him in trouble,
> I will deliver him and honor him.
> With long life I will satisfy him
> and show him my salvation.'"
> **(Psalm 91: 14-16)**

The second revelation occurred when my mom finally came over to tell me and my husband what had happened the morning of the accident. I prayed beforehand that the Lord would rain down His mercy, forgiveness, and compassion before she told us.

This is what happened: She was tired that morning after praying through the night and figured, if they ate some breakfast she would be okay to drive home. The church catered for the event, but the breakfast line was way too long so she decided to stop and get some breakfast on her way home. The church was at least about thirty minutes from her house, so she stopped at Hardee's, which was my daughter's favorite place, to get the famous shaved ham biscuit. The Holy Spirit told her to eat inside and get some coffee instead of using the drive-thru. However, my mom was very tired and decided to use the drive-thru because it was quicker and she wanted to get home to sleep. That was a wrong decision because, as the Word says, obedience to the voice of the Lord is better than any sacrifice (1Samuel 15:22). She got the food and my daughter ate it quickly, then went straight to sleep. My mom knew this because she looked back in the mirror of her car and saw Kiara sleeping.

My mom kept driving and when she was close to her house, two blocks away to be exact, she thought that she had made it home but she had fallen asleep at the wheel. She woke up in severe pain and saw a tree in her face and then realized that she never made it home but fell asleep and hit a tree in the park by her house. The guy who saw the accident from afar off, who was about half mile in front of her coming from the opposite direction, said that he saw a car swerving out of control. He sped up to see what was going on but when he caught up to her, she had already hit the tree. He immediately came to her aid but she kept saying, "Just get my baby!" When she had gained consciousness, she had called out my daughter's name and Kiara had answered her but then there was silence. The man looked in the back and said, "I don't see anyone." My daughter was lying down so he couldn't see her easily. He finally found her and got her out of the car and, as he did so, he felt her take her last breath — in his arms.

While my mom was telling us what had happened, I asked her, "Why didn't you call me or Stepdad to come and pick you guys up because we had rested?" She then told us that she was angry with him because he had suggested that they leave when he left the night of the prayer, around the same time I left, so that he could trail her home and make sure they made it back safely.

My husband and I were stunned. It's so important to hear and obey the voice of the Lord. She had two chances to choose to listen to the prompting from the Holy Spirit but did her own thing instead; something that we all do at some time or other in our lives. This choice cost her severe heartache and pain, and a serious breakdown in her marriage and our relationship. Not because I was holding anything against her but she could not forgive herself and she distanced herself from me. I think she was reminded of the accident when she was around me because my mom, myself, and Kiara did so many things together and now my daughter was no longer part of our trio.

I thank God that after she shared her devastating story, my husband said to me that he felt so sorry for her because she had to live with the consequences of her choices that night. He said, "I am going to be praying for her because that has got to be so hard on her knowing how she felt about our precious little girl." I saw the look in her eyes as she spoke to us and immediately I said, "I forgive you, Momma." That was what God was calling me to do. She said, "Thank you so much, but how do I forgive myself?" I replied, "That is something that only God can help you with because it will have to be 'Not by might nor by power, but by My Spirit, Says the Lord of hosts' (Zechariah 4:6). In the same way that I allowed God to carry me through this tragic situation, you must allow Him to do the same for you. You have to repent for not being obedient to God's instructions and ask for His forgiveness. Forgive yourself and allow the Holy Spirit to comfort your heart, and keep your mind stayed on the Lord so He can keep you in perfect peace."

> **"'Come now, let us settle the matter,'**
> **says the Lord.**
> **'Though your sins are like scarlet,**
> **they shall be as white as snow;**
> **though they are red as crimson,**
> **they shall be like wool.'"**
> **(Isaiah 1:18)**

This third revelation is the one that I pray will bless all those who have lost children. I hope it will help them to understand the God we serve and how much He truly is the epitome of love. I went back to God and asked Him why my daughter didn't get up and live again, especially when I had so much faith in Him that I *had* to believe that it could happen. He told me, it wasn't because of my lack of faith. This is what He said to me:

"She chose to stay with Me. Remember when you, your cousin and her husband were praying for her to get up and the table was shaking? She was in the middle of

making her decision and, when everything stopped moving, she had decided to stay with Me. Remember when you were dreaming about her? I told you that she loved you, her dad, her baby sister who she had waited so long for, and your entire family so much, but there was not anything on Earth that you could give her that can compare to being in the Presence of the Lord. She was a child who knew Me and when her decision time came, she chose to stay with Me.

Remember, I told you to bask in the glory of knowing that you raised her in the admonition of the Lord. This was because she chose to stay with Me."

So for those of you who cannot understand why some children die so young, it is because in their valley of decision they are approached by a loving God to come with Him — and they go. Just know that they are in the best hands they could ever be in. We love them with all of our hearts but there truly is nothing like the Presence of the Lord. Ask me how

I know? Through all the processes in my life, I have tasted and seen that He is good because He carried me through all these trials and tribulations, and today I love Him more than anything.

By the way, when He says He will confirm His Word with signs following (Mark 16:20, NKJV), be sure that He will. A short while later, someone from my church who was believing with me for my daughter to get up and live, called me crying because she said she asked God why Kiara didn't get up and He told her because she chose to stay with Him! That's the loving God we serve. He will show anyone who is believing for anything and waiting for an answer, why things happen — in His timing.

Our God is so awesome like that because He wants us to get understanding from everything that we go through in life. Know that the Lord loves us and He never said that life would be a bed of roses all the time. He said we would have trials and tribulations.

He knows how our lives will end but what we should focus on is how we live this life and how we represent Him in the process. Do we fall apart every time something happens that we are unprepared for? What would happen if we trusted Him to lead us and guide us into all truth as His Word says? What would life be like if we allowed Him to be our present help in our times of trouble?

I know the answer to all these questions and it is that life will be full of ups and downs but, in the end, we are stronger and wiser and can conquer the storms because He has given us the ability by *His* power and might and not ours. The Spirit of the Lord is our teacher and guide, and we have to allow Him access to our lives for Him to be able to be the Lord of all. He will not violate your will, so give Him full access to do what He wills because He truly wants what's best for us at the end of the day. He knows what your expected end is, so why not trust Him with your life and see if He can do something better with it than we ever could? He truly wants to carry ALL of your grief and sorrows, so why not let Him because He never sleeps nor slumbers. Rest in the fact that He knows all and sees all, so He can see what we cannot. Trust that if He calls you to it, He will bring you through it with the victory.

The victory belongs to Jesus and through every test and trial, we have become stronger and better for having gone through the process of losing a child and we can help the next person because we have been through what they are going through. As the Word says in 2 Corinthians 5:8, "We are confident, yes, well pleased rather to be absent from the body and to be present with the Lord." That is where our precious children are and He loves them with an unconditional love. They are well taken care of with Him, trust me.

I remember one particular time I was at a praise and worship service and as I was praising the Lord, I saw my daughter — dressed in all white — and she said to me, "Momma, I'm all right and I am having so much fun here so don't worry about me. I love you so much," and then she went away. That did my heart so much good because I was not worried if she was all right, but I just missed her so much and my loving God let me see that vision because He loved me beyond anything I could ever imagine.

I pray this blesses you and gives you the hope that can only be found in Jesus. Allow Him access into your heart and let Him mend it and fix all of the broken places, to get you to the place where you let Him carry all of the grief and sorrow — and you begin to live again.

Hope & Healing

There is so much power in praise and I think people don't realize just how much. When you praise your way through, it is so liberating. Praise opens up a dialogue between you and the Father where you reverence Him and tell Him how wonderful, gracious, and merciful He is; and He, in return, shows you that He is all that, and so much more. God inhabits the praises of His people because as much as it is for Him, it also makes your heart warm to Him. When you sing about His goodness, it ignites a fire in your heart and you want to raise your hands and even dance before Him just like David danced. Then the worship that you do, sitting at His feet and absorbing all that He is, makes you feel like you are in Heaven because in His presence, there is fullness of joy and peace. There truly is nothing like the presence of the Lord.

Now, after you praise and worship Him, quieten your heart before Him and let Him pour back into you. He always wants to have two-way communication with His children, the same way we want to with our children. He will give you instructions for your life and even just wrap you in His arms and love you in a sense. He is a good and loving Father and wants to lead and guide you into all the truth and He does that when you give Him your ear, without distractions and noise.

> **"The Lord your God in your midst,**
> **The Mighty One, will save;**
> **He will rejoice over you with gladness,**
> **He will quiet *you* with His love,**
> **He will rejoice over you with singing."**
> **(Zephaniah 3:17)**

What can I say about this thing called forgiveness? It is pivotal in you being delivered from so many things. When we are unable to forgive, it causes us to become bitter instead of better. God cannot work on your behalf except to help you get rid of all unforgiveness. It is a blessing blocker and causes all kinds of physical, mental, and emotional issues for the one who will not forgive. Forgiveness is a choice and, in my choice to forgive all that God had instructed me to, I was able to walk in the liberty and freedom that only comes from Him. Deliverance is a choice and I chose to be free from everything that was holding me back through unforgiveness.

Chapter 7

The Triumph

> **"Blessed be the God and Father of our Lord Jesus Christ, the Father of mercies and God of all comfort, who comforts us in all our tribulation, that we may be able to comfort those who are in any trouble, with the comfort with which we ourselves are comforted by God."**
>
> **(2 Corinthians 1:3-4)**

After a week of relaxation and rest from the process of laying my Kiara to rest, I returned back to my normal life and had to face returning to her school without her because I was caring for my little cousin who was in the preschool program at the same school.

I prayed before we left because this was a hard thing for me but I faced it head on with God on my side and drove to the school. I said, "Lord, you got me, right?" The preschoolers had to be signed in daily, so I took my little cousin and my baby out of the car and we walked towards the school building. I felt as if everyone was staring at me but I signed her into her classroom and went back out to my car. I cried and said, "Thank you, Lord. I did it."

As the days went by, it became easier because I allowed God to help me each day. When I was at the school, I didn't even think about getting Kiara's things from her desk. But one day, the school principal brought them to me and proceeded to tell me that he also lost his son tragically and that he knew how I felt. I was in awe and we talked a little about how he coped and I told him, "I have God on my side and that's how I'm coping." We agreed that God is the best being to have on our side as we cope with life's challenges and losses.

The Triumph

That year, in the school yearbook, they had a tribute to Kiara on the first page and a student wrote a poem about her. My heart was so touched. Kiara's third-grade class also wrote individual letters to me and I thought that was so awesome of her teacher to have them do that — I still have every single letter.

There was one thing that kept me bound for a while, and that was driving. Every time I got behind the wheel, I would experience panic attacks even though I had never had an accident. The thought of me falling asleep while driving, was always at the forefront of my mind because that's what happened in Kiara's case. Sometimes, I would get ready to go somewhere and would drive for five minutes down the road when, all of a sudden, I would become sleepy and I would then turn around and go back home because I did not want to fall asleep and harm myself or my baby girl, or anyone else on the road. This went on for about eight months because the devil knew of my situation and wanted to torment me with it. Finally, after missing out on so many events or even normal outings, I decided to ask the Lord to help me. He told me to keep my mind stayed on Him, to keep the Word of God at the forefront of my mind, and to speak to the situation and command that spirit of fear to go. I would pray, "God's Word says He has not given me the spirit of fear but of power, love, and a sound mind." So, as I began to pray this every day, I was able to conquer the fear and move past it. I was able to drive wherever I wanted to and whenever I wanted to.

"For God has not given us a spirit of fear, but of power and of love and of a sound mind." (2 Timothy 1:7)

I also had trouble allowing other people to drive my baby girl somewhere. If I allowed anyone to, I would call them constantly. I had it in my mind that if they had a problem with me calling, then they would not have that privilege anymore. God showed me that that was fear rearing its ugly head again. He revealed to me that I needed to cast it down, and trust that when I prayed over her when she was with others, that my prayers would not be hindered because of that fear. This was also a process and the fear played in my head for quite a while because I did not cast those thoughts down. It caused me to cling to my baby girl and not allow anyone to care for her but myself. People would ask if they could give me a break and I would immediately say, "No, thank you. I don't want a break," even though I knew, I probably needed one. I did not let her go with anyone for a while because I had to get to that place where I had confidence and could trust that she would be safe. God finally gave me victory in this area too!

**"Be anxious for nothing, but in everything
by prayer and supplication,
with thanksgiving, let your requests
be made known to God;
and the peace of God,**

**which surpasses all understanding, will guard your hearts and minds through Christ Jesus."
(Philippians 4:6 – 7)**

It seemed like after Kiara's passing, I started to notice a lot of children dying in car accidents and I would immediately pray for their families. I would always pray for the peace that surpasses all understanding because I found that when you tried to understand why immediately, then you would take your mind to a place where you could not get it together and function in a rational manner. I would see people so distraught and hysterical and I would pray for them because I could feel their pain and I knew that feeling all too well.

Having lost a child myself allowed me to pray from a different place to those who pray and really don't know what it is like to lose a child. I prayed from a place of compassion that went deeper than the surface — my prayers were heartfelt. I would pray in the Spirit for the families because it is a tough process to go through; but with God, all things are possible and there is healing from sorrow and grief that has to take place.

I know that you have to grieve but don't let it take years because that is not God's plan, so here are some Scriptures on overcoming sorrow and grief that you can pray over yourself or anyone going through the loss of a child, a loved one, or any type of sorrow or grief — no matter the reason.

Matthew 5:4

"Blessed are those who mourn, For they shall be comforted."

2 Corinthians 1:3-4

"Blessed be the God and Father of our Lord Jesus Christ, the Father of mercies and God of all comfort, who comforts us in all our tribulation, that we may be able to comfort those who are in any trouble, with the comfort with which we ourselves are comforted by God."

Psalm 46:1-2

"God is our refuge and strength, A very present help in trouble. Therefore we will not fear, Even though the earth be removed, And though the mountains be carried into the midst of the sea;"

Psalm 119:50

"This is my comfort in my affliction, For Your word has given me life."

Romans 8:18

"For I consider that the sufferings of this present time are not worthy to be compared with the glory which shall be revealed in us."

2 Corinthians 7:10

"For godly sorrow produces repentance leading to

salvation, not to be regretted; but the sorrow of the world produces death."

Psalm 18:2

"The Lord is my rock and my fortress and my deliverer; My God, my strength, in whom I will trust; My shield and the horn of my salvation, my stronghold."

Psalm 73:26

My flesh and my heart fail; But God is the strength of my heart and my portion forever."

Psalm 34:18-19

"The Lord is near to those who have a broken heart And saves such as have a contrite spirit. Many are the afflictions of the righteous, But the Lord delivers him out of them all."

Matthew 11:28

"Come to Me, all you who labor and are heavy laden, and I will give you rest."

Psalm 147:3

"He heals the brokenhearted And binds up their wounds."

Joshua 1:9

"Have I not commanded you? Be strong and of good courage; do not be afraid, nor be dismayed, for the Lord your God is with you wherever you go."

John 14:1

"Let not your heart be troubled; you believe in God, believe also in Me,"

Revelation 21:4

"And God will wipe away every tear from their eyes, there shall be no more death, nor sorrow, nor crying. There shall be no more pain, for the former things have passed away."

1 Peter 5:6-7

"Therefore humble yourselves under the mighty

hand of God, that he may exalt you in due time, casting all your care upon Him, for he cares for you."

Psalm 22:24

"For He has not despised nor abhorred the affliction of the afflicted; Nor has He hidden His face from Him; But when He cried to Him, He heard.

Hope & Healing

God carried me through this entire journey from tragedy to triumph. It is a true testament to the God we serve who is everything and more to me because He showed me His faithfulness in the most tangible ways. I was able to do things that I know were all at His remarkable hand. The person that people saw me be during this time was all because of His everlasting love, His grace that was so sufficient for me, and His mercies that were new every morning.

My prayer is that you will know that God is so good in the midst of our storms and that He loves us so much. He is a God of love in its purest form. The Bible tells us that God is faithful to perform His Word and not ours, so I encourage you to pray the Scriptures over your situations and circumstances to see God's hand moving over those situations, circumstances, and your life. I had the Word working on my behalf because I was speaking the Word only because I wanted God's Will to be done and I knew His Will was to see me walk in victory over this tragedy and not have it take me to depression and despair like the devil wanted it to.

When we understand that in Christ Jesus we have the victory over the enemy and all his tricks and tactics that he uses to distract us from the focus of God's plan for our lives, then we truly see and show the world that God is who we need to get through it all. God is who His Word says He is: all-powerful, all-knowing, and present everywhere — nothing happens without His knowledge. We understand that all things work together for our good and He never said we would not go through trials and tribulations but through Him, we can make it through them. With God, all things are possible and without God, things can be impossible.

Know God — know peace, strength, and joy.
No God — no peace, strength, and joy.

Conclusion

**"Trust in the Lord with all your heart,
And lean not on your own understanding;
In all your ways acknowledge Him,
And He shall direct your paths."
(Proverbs 3:5-6)**

This passage of Scripture should be the building block of what you do before anything else in order to get deliverance from the sorrow and grief that you are feeling because of the loss of your child. Trust and believe that the Lord is your way out and nothing else.

I went through this process from tragedy to triumph, with the Lord right by my side and that's the only way I made it through with the victory. The Lord God Almighty carried me through this with the peace that surpassed all of mine and everyone's understanding. It was only because of His grace, mercy, and love that I am able to write this book to help you out. It is nothing so great about me but everything so amazing about Him. He loves you so much that He wants you to see Him be God to someone who went through what you are going through; and because He carried them — they were victorious.

If you have gone through a tragedy and you can't get past the hurt and pain, know that God wants you to let Him be God and carry you to a place of healing and hope. First and foremost, forgive yourself for not allowing Him to help you and love you through this process because, for some, you blame Him for what happened knowingly or unknowingly. God does not come to kill, steal, or destroy; that's the devil's job. He came so that we could have life and have it more abundantly. If you are angry with God then go to Him and tell Him how you really feel. Don't hold it in and let that anger fester because it will make your body and soul sick. Tell Him about it and then listen to what He has to say concerning your situation. I had questions and He provided me with answers — He will give you the answers too, in His timing.

> **"He heals the brokenhearted**
> **and binds up their wounds."**
> **(Psalm 147:3)**

For those of you who may be reading this and you don't know Jesus, then I encourage you to accept Him as your personal Lord and Savior. Pray Romans 10:9-10 that says: "that if you confess with your mouth the Lord Jesus and believe in your heart that God has raised Him from the dead, you will be saved. For with the heart, one believes unto righteousness, and with the mouth, confession is made unto salvation." I pray that you make this confession and watch the Lord show up and heal your broken heart and change your life for the better. Allow Him to do it for you today! No matter what trials and tribulations life throws at you, going to God is the only place where you can release your hurt and pain in a way that is helpful and not harmful to you and everyone affected by the loss of a child.

> **"Trust in Him at all times, you people;**
> **Pour out your heart before Him;**
> **God *is* a refuge for us."**
> **(Psalm 62:8)**

Through this tragedy of losing my child, God took me through the process of forgiving and releasing my pain to Him. He gave me the heart to forgive my dad for abandoning me. The Lord helped me forgive my stepdad for how he treated my mom and our family, my mother for allowing him into our lives when he wasn't loving or kind towards us, and for not yielding to the Holy Spirit when He told her His instructions the day of the accident. I was also able to forgive my husband for betraying our marriage covenant with infidelity. I found that as I was able to forgive, God took me from grace to glory.

> **"If we claim to have fellowship with him
> and yet walk in the darkness,
> we lie and do not live out the truth.
> But if we walk in the light, as he is in the light,
> we have fellowship with one another, and the
> blood of Jesus, his Son, purifies us from all sin."
> (1 John 1:6-7)**

The unforgiveness was holding me back from operating at my full potential. The unforgiveness was tied to my unhappiness and rendered me unholy. I was not a whole person because I was not operating in the Kingdom principle of forgiving others, so that my Father in Heaven could forgive me. How could I walk in unforgiveness and still confess to be following God and walking in the light? Because He is a forgiving God, so I had to be as well.

I had to give God the pains of my past in order to walk into my future that was so bright but I could not see it because of the darkness of not being able to forgive. It had me bound and not free. Now that the Son has set me free from what was holding me back, now I can be all that He created me to be. I can now be a vessel that He can use for His Kingdom and glory.

Lastly, He took me through the process of forgiving myself for walking in fear when my God has said, that's not the Spirit that He has given me. My God says that He has given me the Spirit of power, love, and a sound mind and that His perfect love casts out all fear, so I should not walk in fear but in faith in Him. If you walk in fear, then you are not walking in faith because fear and faith don't mix. My advice to you is, don't do things in fear — do all things in faith, to the glory of God.

Trust in the Lord with all your heart because He is trustworthy! This is the lesson I have spent my whole life trying to get right but I have always gotten in my own way because I felt I had a better or faster way, but my God has been patient with me. In the end, His ways are higher than ours so let His Will be done so you don't have to go through the same unnecessary situations as I did.

Through all the trials and tribulations of my life, one thing I know is that God will carry you in His loving arms and mend your broken heart like no other. Let His Will be done in your life and allow Him to be there for you as He was and is always with me. With Jesus, there is liberty and freedom, and deliverance that only comes from Him.

The Bible says in John 8:36: **"Therefore if the Son makes you free, you shall be free indeed."** Your deliverance can happen today, right now when you choose the Father, Son, and Holy Spirit to be the head of your life and lead and guide you to all truth.
Blessings be unto you!

Steps to Turn Tragedy into Triumph

Cast your cares on the Lord because He cares for you.

Pray without ceasing.

Praise and worship the Lord daily.

Read the Bible daily.

Study the Scriptures on grief and sorrow.

Sit quietly after praise and prayer to hear instructions from the Lord on what to do.

Tell God *exactly* how you feel. Pour out your heart to Him because He loves you.

Have a heart to forgive every person, even yourself.

Allow yourself time to grieve but don't let it be forever.

Pray some more.

Acknowledgements

I want to thank my husband, Kirk, for being my rock through this entire process because you made all the arrangements when my mind could not comprehend that I was planning my baby girl's funeral.

To Verrick and Mecheco Norwood, what can I say about you two? You flew in from California on a day's notice and prayed over my baby girl, Kiara, and we witnessed the hand of God. I am eternally grateful that I shared that experience with you two.

To Tamela Wynn, my other half who protected me like no other and was lovingly called Code Texas because you did not let anyone come to me with ANYTHING — you are my greatest supporter. You know the bond we share is such a gift to my life and you know how I feel about you, so it goes without saying.

To my St. Louis Christian Center family, I am so grateful that you showed our family so much love during the memorial service and repass, and for all the encouraging words and expressions of love.

To Pastor and Minister Horry, the message and the music brought so much light to the fact that without God in your life, things could be a mess; but He can turn it around to a message of His love and the hope we must have in Him to get through any situation. You both blessed my entire family and my friends' lives.

To Pastor Myrten and Toni Byrd, you know that you hold a special place in my heart for standing and believing with me for Kiara to rise and walk in the Name of Jesus and for praying with me at the funeral home.

To Minister Tina Hill, thank you for the Obituary program that you did when we just dropped off some photo albums and said, "Go for it" and you did an amazing job.

To Jytone Johnson, for making my angel look so adorable by doing her hair and getting her dressed. You know where we stand to this day because you did that!

To Kesha Taylor and Verneda Rogers, thank you for getting her clothing items for me. You guys rock!

To Kim Yancey, thank you for getting me together with my hair and taking me to see my mom in the hospital.

To my dear friend, Mary Hammons, thank you for getting my outfit I wore for the service and hanging with me when I couldn't even fathom that I was going through this process. You kept me talking and laughing at a time when I didn't think there was anything to laugh about.

To Mattie Spearman, my grandmother in love, thank you for checking on my mom throughout the entire process when I know it was difficult for you and your family as well.

To my dear Aunt Robin Williams, thank you for taking care of Mom after the accident. Your love and care helped carry all of us through that difficult time.

To Loretta Harvey, thank you for checking on me daily and for the love you sent my way by saying, "Just take a bite of something to eat to keep your strength."

To the Nursery Department of SLCC, you guys know you rock because you stood with me, and the outpouring of love was amazing and showed the strength of us as a true family and not just a ministry team.

To Tyrese and Tina Cooper, thank you for bringing the video of the Children's Ministry at the All Night Intercessory Prayer because I saw that my daughter was having lots of fun. Hers was the first face you see in the video and it gave me such joy to see it.

To all my family and friends that sent me love, cards, gifts, and prayers, thank you from the bottom of my heart.

To the staff and students at William Holliday Elementary School, thank you for the cards and encouraging words.

To Minister Catherine Storing (my writing mama), for teaching me everything I needed to know to write a book and shared with me all of your top secrets to getting the job done.

I thank Gaylena White for the WWM21 program that brought me to a new place in Christ because we walked with you as you walked with Christ. I was able to experience the Trinity in such a profound way after spending much time at the feet of Jesus and constantly in the Word. It helped me with this writing process.

I thank Sophia Ruffin for teaching the *Complete the Book in 10 Days* webinar that gave me the confidence to believe in myself as a writer and started this whole writing process for me.

I thank Kimberly Jones for teaching me the importance of decreeing and declaring the Word of God over my life and seeing the Word work as I worked the Word.

I thank my husband Kirk Thompson for bearing with me as I took on this challenge of writing this book and dealing with the emotions it took to accomplish this task of helping others get through this tough situation of losing a child but doing it with God.

I thank my daughters who had to sacrifice time with me as I wrote this book to deliver the people of God from sorrow and grief of the loss of a child, but I will make sure to make it up to them and my husband with some much-needed family time.

Without every person that I thanked above, this book would not have been possible. Thank you, Lord, for staying on me to get this book out and giving me the ability to write it in such a way that will bring deliverance to Your people through my obedience to You to tell how You brought me through with my mind, peace, joy, strength, and love.

About the Author

Pamela Thompson is a native of Centreville, Illinois. She is the wife of Kirk Thompson, her husband of 20 years, a mother of three daughters, and a woman of faith. Pamela has an Associate Degree in Marketing Management from Belleville Area College. She is an inspiration to her family, friends, members of her church's youth group, prayer team, and her community at large.

This book was birthed out of the process God took her through, to free her from the sorrow and grief that tried to bind her after losing her eight-year-old daughter in a car accident. Through God's grace, Pamela hopes that this book inspires every reader to seek the Lord when trials and tribulations come up in their lives. She is determined to go out into the entire world and preach the gospel with Holy boldness to all who God is calling her to.

Pamela currently resides in Brentwood, California where she is an active participant and prayer warrior in the lives of her husband and children, and at The Rock Church where she serves faithfully.

Contact the Author

https://www.facebook.com/PamelaThompson

Author Page on Facebook

@PamelaMoniqueThompson

https://Twitter.com/@PamelaMThompson

https://www.instagram.com/Godchild529

https://LinkedIn.com/PamelaThompson

www.pamelamthompson.com

www.ingramcontent.com/pod-product-compliance
Lightning Source LLC
Chambersburg PA
CBHW070608010526
44118CB00012B/1470